Greater Love
Through Suffering
and Sacrifice

Greater Love Through Suffering and Sacrifice

GEORGE E PFAUTSCH

authorHOUSE®

AuthorHouse™ LLC
1663 Liberty Drive
Bloomington, IN 47403
www.authorhouse.com
Phone: 1-800-839-8640

Published by AuthorHouse   01/16/2014

ISBN: 978-1-4918-5389-4 (sc)
ISBN: 978-1-4918-5392-4 (e)

Library of Congress Control Number: 2014901131

DEDICATION

In March, 2013, I lost a dear friend and cousin, Sister Mary Paul Pfautsch. Sister Mary Paul lived the title of this book. She joined the Sisters of St. Francis of Perpetual Adoration  in Mishawaka, Indiana in 1948, and then became a teacher for the Order until 1962. In 1962 she went to the Philippines with three other Sisters and founded what today is the Immaculate Conception Province of the Sisters of St. Francis of Perpetual Adoration. She served as the first Provincial Superior from 1993 until 1998. Sister Mary Paul dedicated her entire life to serving our Lord.

Even though many miles separated us, she sometimes served as an editor and advisor to me. Of far greater importance, she was a cherished friend. She was a perpetually cheerful person, even through times of great suffering and sacrifice. She will be greatly missed by all of us who were fortunate enough to know her.

CONTENTS

OTHER BOOKS
BY
GEORGE E PFAUTSCH

Redefining Morality
A Threat to our Nation

Time of Greatness
Morality Matters

Flawed Justice
When our Unalienable Right are Ignored

The Purpose of Life
Know Him, Love Him, Serve Him

The Wisdom of our Soul

A Case of Modern Day Pharisees
The Need for Holiness

The Transformation of America
As Government Grows—Liberty Yields

Hey Kids, Want Some Chocolates?
My Family's Journey to Freedom
(co-authored with Melitta Strandberg)

A Man From Two Worlds
(co-authored with Leroy New)

INTRODUCTION

During our life on earth we are witnesses to much suffering and pain. Our normal view of suffering and pain is one that centers on the physical aspects of such suffering. Sometimes we also think of the suffering and pain caused by mental anguish. Much has been written of such suffering and pain.

It is not often that we think of the greater love that can be achieved from suffering and pain during our lives on earth. Rather, we are inclined to pray to our Lord to relieve the suffering and pain of those who are experiencing it and that is an appropriate way to express our love of our fellow human beings and indicate our desire that their pain may be diminished.

But suffering, pain and sacrifice can also be endured as a means to demonstrate a greater love of our Lord and of one another. We have no greater demonstration of that than the passion of our Lord who through his suffering and pain demonstrated the greatest love of us that could possibly be demonstrated by God himself. Jesus did not need to suffer death for us. He suffered his passion and death to show us that no greater love can take place than to lay down one's life for another. His whole life was a demonstration of his great love and great mercy for every individual on earth.

His life was also more than just that great demonstration of his love for us. The sacrifice of assuming a human nature that our Lord would make for each of us through his incarnation was also the greatest display of humility known to mankind. Our Lord did not come to earth to the blare of trumpets and birth in a royal palace. Rather, he came to earth in a manger and lived the life of a carpenter. God could have come to us in any form He wished, but He wished to show us the value of humility. He would then experience his passion and death to show us the apex of love for us and how we can demonstrate that love for one another.

It was through his own humility that He would also show us its importance in achieving a greater love for one another and by achieving a greater love for one another we would also be achieving a greater love of Him. In doing that, He would show us the way to observe the only two commandments He gave us; to love Him above all else and to love one another as we love our self.

Following his glorious ascension and his return to Heaven to be seated at the right hand of the Father, He would permit many of his most faithful followers to also experience suffering and pain. Through that suffering and pain they demonstrated their great love for Him.

He would ask all of us during our time on earth to also be willing to sacrifice the things of this world to gain a greater place with Him in eternity. The purpose of this book is to note how suffering and pain while on earth can lead to a greater love of our Creator.

CHAPTER 1

THE LIFE AND SUFFERING OF JESUS

The Word made Flesh is a great mystery. It is also the greatest example to mankind of humility and love, which is unparalleled by any other human beings. It is very likely that most of us, when we focus on the passion of our Lord think about whether or not we have anything close to the capability to love Him as He loved us. His entire life was devoted to the love of us.

His life and his love of mankind began in a lowly manger. His Incarnation is impossible for us to fully fathom and appreciate. This tiny child in the manger was the 2nd Person of the Blessed Trinity—the Son of God. He was our eternal God and yet he chose for our sake to dwell among us. Why did he choose to humble Himself in this lowly manner? Those who were expecting a Messiah were expecting a mighty human who would rid them of their persecutors. But his mission on earth was a far different mission. His whole life would be dedicated to the salvation of mankind. His lowly birth would be the ultimate example of how humility should matter to each of us.

The world would know little of the early years of this Person who was our Savior. We relate to Him more easily because He became one of us. But even though He was one of us He was also God. One of the few things we know of Him in his early years on earth was his teaching in the temple as a young boy. It would be the only indication from Him in his early years on earth of someone who possessed more than just a human nature.

Before demonstrating his great love for us by dying for our sins, He would spend three years as the greatest teacher and moral philosopher to have walked the face of the earth. He would spend those three years providing us with the information we need to spend eternity with Him. Everything He taught us was a furtherance of the two great commandments He gave us. He would tell us that our primary purpose on earth was to love Him with all our heart, soul, mind and strength and to love our neighbor as our self. His teachings would be delivered in a manner that would withstand the passing of time.

During the three years before He died for us, He would give those with Him numerous indications that He would die and then arise to demonstrate his great mercy and love for us. It was difficult for his apostles to understand what He was saying to them and it still is hard for us on earth today to fully comprehend it.

One of our chores on earth is to spend more time attempting to fully understand his great love and mercy for us.

If He had so desired, Jesus could have ascended into Heaven before his passion and death for us and been perfectly justified in saying that if we followed everything He taught us while on earth we would live the type of life that is required to be with Him for all eternity. He did not need to go beyond those teachings. But our Lord understood us far better than we understand ourselves. Once before He had set free the entire Jewish people from slavery at the hands of the Egyptians only to see an ungrateful people turn away from Him time after time.

Yes, before his death and passion He could have said that if we took to heart his teachings He would forgive our transgressions and let us join Him after our death on earth. But He knew and understood the weakness of mankind and that a greater display of his mercy for us was necessary to make us better understand how much He loved us. It would also demonstrate to those with faith in Him that his total commitment to love us even unto death must also require a commitment on our part to love Him in return. It was through his passion and death that He exhibited mercy and love that would be impossible for us to replicate.

It is proper and right for each of us to frequently reflect on the passion and death of our Lord and to better understand how they demonstrated the greatest love imaginable for each and every one of us on earth. We will follow the Sorrowful mysteries of the Rosary in the contemplation of his mercy for all of us.

THE AGONY IN THE GARDEN AND JESUS IS CONDEMNED TO DEATH—It is a matter of Christian doctrine that Jesus "suffered under Pontius Pilate". After spending time in the Garden of Gethsemane on Holy Thursday evening He was arrested there following the betrayal of Judas Iscariot. He was then taken before the Jewish leaders. He was mocked, insulted and beaten and eventually turned over to Pilate, the Roman procurator. His "greatest" wrong was to acknowledge that He was the Son of God.

As Christians we often wonder how such a flimsy accusation could have led to the condemnation of death upon a cross. We castigate the Jewish high priests, the Sanhedrin and Pilate in what they did but it was all of us, through our sins, that caused his death. He in his infinite mercy for all of us laid down his life for all of us. He accepted condemnation for all of us so we might have the opportunity for eternal salvation.

As sinful human beings, filled with far too much self-interest, it is very difficult for us to comprehend that someone who had no guilt could love us so much that He would die for us. No greater love could be demonstrated than his willingness to accept death for our sins.

JESUS IS SCOURGED AT THE PILLAR—It was not just a routine death that Jesus would accept for all of us. It was a death preceded by great suffering. After his condemnation He was turned over to executioners who tied Him to a pillar and began taunting and torturing Him. A scourging at the hands of his executioners would be a fearful prelude to the death He would incur.

Such beatings could tear flesh from the body and for many they could have caused death. But He endured them quietly on our behalf. How would we, if innocent of any crime, have endured such pain? Most likely we would have screamed about our innocence and hated those who unjustly punished us. But Jesus did neither. He endured it so one day we might be with Him in Heaven.

JESUS IS CROWNED WITH THORNS—In Mark's gospel, Chapter 15, verses 16 through 20 we are told of the painful events of this phase of Jesus' suffering. *The soldiers led Him away inside the palace, that is, the praetorium, and assembled the whole cohort. They clothed Him in purple and weaving a crown of thorns, placed it on Him. They began to salute Him with "Hail, King of the Jews!" and kept striking his head with a reed and spitting upon Him. They knelt before Him in homage. And when they had mocked Him, they stripped Him of the purple cloak, dressed Him in his own clothes, and led Him out to crucify Him.*

The passion of Jesus went beyond terrible suffering. He would be mocked and spat upon. He would endure the worst of humiliations and He did it for each of us. Even though He endured it for us, there are far, far too many in our world today that do not even acknowledge his existence. Beyond that there are far, far too many who do not acknowledge his great love and mercy for us. What more could He do to show us how much He loved us.

JESUS CARRIES THE CROSS—Of the four gospels, it is Luke's which provides the longest narrative of The Way of the Cross. *As they led Him away they took hold of a certain Simon, a Cyrenian, who was coming in from the country: and after laying the cross on him, they made him carry it behind Jesus. A large crowd of people followed Jesus, including many women who mourned and lamented Him. Jesus turned to them and said, "Daughters of Jerusalem, do not weep for me; weep instead for yourselves and for your children, for indeed, the days are coming when people will say, 'Blessed are the barren, the wombs that never bore and the breasts that never nursed. At that time people will say to the mountains, 'Fall upon us !' and to the hills, 'Cover us!' for if these things are done when the wood is green what will happen when it is dry?" Now two others, both criminals, were led away with him to be executed.*

These words of Jesus are not the easiest words of the Gospel to interpret. Jesus was indicating that He did not just want outward signs of pity, and that it would be wise to save the tears for our own transgressions. Even as Jesus is about to suffer death for us He also seems to be telling us that we too will be expected to suffer and sacrifice. Through his passion and death He clearly demonstrated his love and mercy for mankind, but He too was saying that mankind would need to suffer and sacrifice if we are to be prepared to find a place with Him in eternity. Jesus suffered most of his passion in silence but gave the women a few words that all of us need to ponder.

Sacrifice is a word that in recent years has lost some meaning. In the world today, it is too easy to say that Jesus loves me and I love Him and leave it at that. But that is not what He is telling us. Our love of Him must be more than just words. In order to truly love another, it is necessary to sacrifice our own desires for Him and for our fellow human beings. We must love one another as He loved and died for us and that type of love requires sacrifice. As He was suffering His passion He was reminding the women of Jerusalem and us that He loved us and his love for us included great suffering and then death upon a cross. To love one another as He loved us is a very high bar.

JESUS IS CRUCIFIED—When Jesus reached Golgotha, where He was to be crucified, He was stripped of his garments and nailed to the cross. Before continuing, this is a good time to pause and spend a few minutes to contemplate the excruciating pain and suffering He endured on our behalf. It was an indication of his great mercy and great love which is almost beyond our comprehension.

Then He was hung on a cross and died for our sins.

No greater love exists than to lay down one's life for another. He did that in a way that bears a great deal of meditation and contemplation by us. His death not only demonstrated his love for mankind but through his suffering and death He also demonstrated that it is through suffering and pain that we on earth can increase our love for Him and for our neighbors.

He wants us to think frequently of his great mercy and his great love for us. By frequently thinking of his passion and death for us we are better able to understand what great love really means. Many of his followers have laid down their life for Him. He does not expect all of us to die for Him but He does expect us to be ready to do so. He does expect us to increase our love for Him through greater sacrifice on his behalf and for the love of our neighbor.

If any of us want an example of the greatest love that is possible we need look no further than the suffering, passion and death our Savior endured for us.

CHAPTER 2

THE LOVE AND SACRIFICE OF OUR BLESSED MOTHER

With her words, "Behold, I am the handmaid of the Lord—May it be done to me according to your word", our Blessed Mother indicated her willingness to dedicate her entire life to doing God's will. In so doing she would endure a life of great sacrifice but also live a life of great love for her Son.

After our Lord was conceived by the Holy Spirit, Mary traveled to the house of her cousin Elizabeth. She would remain with her for about three months. Scripture does not give us all the reasons for the visit, but one may have been for her own protection. In those days, becoming pregnant without a husband could have resulted in being stoned to death. Her acceptance to be the Mother of God came with some personal risks and numerous sacrifices.

Thanks to the visit of an angel, Joseph took Mary as his wife. We can imagine that many rumors circulated about her pregnancy and her subsequent marriage to Joseph. Joseph as well as Mary no doubt had to sacrifice much to accept the role God intended for him.

As Mary was about to deliver they had to travel to Bethlehem for a census and because no inn was available for them, Mary would give birth to our Lord and Savior in a lowly stable.

Her trials and sacrifices were only beginning.

Being forewarned by an angel of Herod's intent to kill all the male children of a certain age in the Bethlehem area, Joseph, Mary and the infant Jesus fled to Egypt, where they essentially lived in exile. We do not know exactly how long they lived in Egypt or exactly where they lived. There is a Coptic Church in Cairo, Abu Serga, which is believed to be in the location where the Holy Family lived while in Egypt.

Herod, it is reported, died sometime around 4 AD so they may have been in Egypt several years, but we do not know with certainty. It no doubt was a stay that required some sacrifice. They were separated from family members and lived in a strange land.

After the death of Herod, they returned to Israel and eventually established a home in Nazareth. The only thing the Bible tells us of those years was the event when Jesus was taken to the temple as a boy and became separated from Mary and Joseph. It is also the first insight we may have to his divinity, as He preached to his elders in the temple.

We know almost nothing about our Blessed Mother during the years the Holy Family lived in Nazareth. We know of the incident just cited when Jesus became separated from the family in the temple. We can also deduct from the passages of the Bible that in all likelihood Joseph died during the years following that event in the temple and prior to the public ministry of Jesus.

Mary, no doubt, sacrificed a great deal for her Son and our Savior during his childhood and youth. He was born under difficult circumstances in a stable. They had to flee to Egypt when he was a small baby. They lived in a foreign land away from family. Her life before his public ministry was one dedicated to the birth and caring of her Son.

After Jesus' public ministry began, our Mother's life remained a life dedicated to our Lord and Savior. Her whole life was a lesson in sacrifice and love. We do know that she was in Cana with Him at a wedding feast when He performed his first miracle. Beyond that occurrence we are not told much of her life during the years of his public ministry.

We also know that she was with Him in Jerusalem during his passion and death. She is noted in the fourth Station of the Cross and is with Him at his death. It must have been an almost unbearable time for the Mother of Jesus. She knew that He was not guilty of any crime, but she also understood that He had to die so all of mankind might have the opportunity for salvation.

At the foot of the Cross she heard some of his last words before his death. She would be entrusted to the care of his disciple John. She would also be with the Apostles when the Holy Spirit appeared to them at the first Pentecost.

As requested by her Son on the Cross, Mary would live with the Apostle John sometime following the Ascension of Jesus into Heaven. We do know that she would live in Ephesus, which today is part of Turkey, in her late years on earth.

Biblicists and other historians are not in agreement as regards the Assumption of Mary into Heaven. Some believe she was taken into Heaven after her death. Others believe she was taken to Heaven while still alive. My own faith leads me to believe the latter view. Because there is reason to believe it is sin that causes the corruptibility of the body and because Mary was born without sin, there is some reason to believe that she may never have been subjected to an earthly death. While this is a matter of appropriate reflection, it is not a matter of Catholic dogma.

Another of the rewards that our Lord may have bestowed on his mother, is that she in all likelihood will not be subjected to the resurrection of the body as will be true for the rest of us. She was born without sin, ascended into Heaven having never committed sin and thus exempt from the need of a Particular or Final Judgment. This, too, is not a matter of Catholic dogma.

If the aforementioned circumstances regarding the Assumption, resurrection of the body and the question of Judgment for the Blessed Mother are not tenets of the Church why are they worth noting? They can provide hours of meditation on the special relationship between our Savior and his mother. It is always a good and valuable expenditure of time to try to understand the perfection of love our Heavenly Mother had for her Son, our Lord and Savior. It is that kind of love that souls in Heaven experience. They are the only examples we have of those on earth who were without sin and thus provide us an example of perfect love.

There are many things Scripture does not tell us about the years of the Holy Family, before the public ministry of Jesus. Once they fled to Egypt we know almost nothing further until the time Jesus was a boy and preaching to the elders in the temple. Because of the circumstances surrounding his birth and the information given to Mary and Joseph by the angels we can assume they understood that their Son was the Messiah, who was awaited by the Jewish people. However, it was not they, who in the Scriptures, proclaimed Him as the Messiah but rather John the Baptist.

As just noted, from the words of Sacred Scripture, we can assume Mary and Joseph knew Jesus was the Messiah. We can also surmise from the miracle at Cana that the Blessed Mother understood at that occasion that her Son was our divine Savior, since she told the wine stewards to do as her Son directed them. She must have had some understanding of his divine nature.

We also do not know what life was like within the home of the Holy Family. We can only try to partially comprehend what it may have been like for the parents of our Savior, when he was a child, a teenager and a young man in his twenties. As a young man he lived the life of a carpenter and probably worked a great deal with Joseph in that trade.

We do not know if, when, or how Jesus may have displayed his divine nature to Mary and Joseph. Given that He came to us in the most humble of ways, it is reasonable to believe He may have made very minimal displays, if any, of his divine nature during those many years. We simply do not know, but these things are also worth mediation time to better understand his majesty and the greatness of our Blessed Mother. He truly did display to us his great humility and love.

Many honors have been bestowed on the Mother of God. As a mother, apostle and disciple, she devoted her entire life on earth to her son. As mother, apostle and disciple she undoubtedly had a love of her Son that is difficult, and maybe impossible, for other human beings to parallel, because she was without sin. She underwent all the sacrifices any other mother would have undergone, but she was called on to do even more. She saw her son suffer and die for us, even though she knew there was no earthly justification for his condemnation. It is difficult to understand the hardship of such sacrifice.

Before her Son was born she left us with the beautiful words of the Magnificat.

My soul proclaims the greatness of the Lord,
my spirit rejoices in God my Savior
for he has looked with favor on his lowly servant.

From this day forward all generations will call me blessed:
the Almighty has done great things for me,
and holy is his name.

He has mercy on those who fear him in every generation.

He has shown the strength of his arm,
he has scattered the proud in their conceit.

He has cast down the mighty from their thrones,
and has lifted up the lowly.

He has filled the hungry with good things,
and the rich he has sent away empty.
He has come to the help of his servant Israel
for he has remembered his promise of mercy,
the promise he made to our fathers,
to Abraham and his children for ever.

This beautiful canticle is attributed to our Holy Mother in Luke's gospel at the time she visited her cousin Elizabeth, which was prior to the birth of Jesus. Her prayer would indicate knowledge of what was in store for her. She has been called blessed for generations. She offered her whole life as a sacrifice for our Savior and is our Co-redemptorist. She is the Queen of Heaven and Earth. She is our model for how we are to love.

CHAPTER 3

ST. JOHN THE BAPTIST

Scripture tells us that St. John the Baptist's life was dedicated to fulfilling his role as Precursor to our Lord and Savior, Jesus Christ. Shortly after her conception by the Holy Spirit, Mary went to visit her cousin, Elizabeth, who at the time was six months pregnant. When Elizabeth greeted Mary, we are told that the child in her womb leapt with joy.

John the Baptist was a special person from the day he was conceived. He was the son of Zechariah, a priest in the Temple of Jerusalem. His mother was Elizabeth, a cousin of the Blessed Virgin Mary. He was an unexpected child to these two, who were elderly when he was conceived. It was the angel, Gabriel, who appeared to Zechariah and told him that his wife would bear a child even though she was beyond the normal child-bearing age.

Scripture also informs us that Zechariah would be struck dumb because he displayed a weakness of faith when told he would father a child at an elderly age. But following the birth of his son he also gave us the beautiful Canticle of Zechariah, which is prayed frequently at morning prayers. This Canticle includes the words spoken to his infant son: *You, my child, shall be called the prophet of the Most High; for you will go before the Lord to prepare his way, to give his people knowledge of salvation by the forgiveness of their sins.*

John would fulfill the words of his father throughout his entire life. As a young man he would live the life of a hermit in the desert lands of Judea. He would begin preaching on the banks of the river, Jordan, against the sins of the time. He would call people to repent for their sins and called on them to do penance. He would baptize many people. Nowhere in Scripture do we find anything about his life that was not done in accordance with the words in his father's canticle.

It was John who recognized Jesus publicly as the Messiah and the Lamb of God. When Jesus came to meet him and to be baptized by John, he spoke these words; "It is I who need baptism from you". When Jesus left the Jordan valley to begin his public life in Galilee, John remained and continued his preaching there.

John did not partake in the material things of life. He lived the life of a hermit and survived from the food he found in the desert. Scripture describes his clothing as made of camel's hair and his food as locust and wild honey. But his simple life also attracted many of the people of the Jordan valley and they accepted him as the prophet and forerunner of the Messiah. His whole life seemed to be dedicated to "give his people knowledge of salvation by the forgiveness of their sins".

John's preaching gathered a number of disciples. Some accounts number his disciples as thirty. Among these were Andrew and his brother Simon who would become the early apostles of our Lord.

John did not mince words. Often the Pharisees and Sadducees would come to listen to him preach. It is not exactly known why they came to hear him because they too thought of themselves as spiritual leaders. When they came John was not reluctant to criticize their too frequent pompous self-righteousness.

Eventually John's criticism of wrongful deeds would cause his imprisonment. During his time, the tetrarch of Perea and Galilee was Herod Antipas, the son of Herod the Great. John denounced his adulterous and incestuous relationship with Herodias, who was also the niece of Herod.

Because of his criticism, Herod had John imprisoned at Machaerus Fortress on the Dead Sea. Although it is thought that Herod over time became somewhat fond of John the same was not true of Herodias who despised him.

Herodias would obtain her revenge following a dance before Herod and others by her daughter, Salome.

When Herod promised her any wish she might ask for, she asked for the head of John on a platter. This wish came at the bequest of her mother, Herodias. Herod regretfully complied with the request and had John beheaded.

When news of John's death reached the apostles, Scripture tells us they recovered his body and buried him. Scripture also makes another reference by Jesus about the greatness of John the Baptist.

When Jesus heard of the death of John, he had the following to say about him. *No one born of woman is greater than John, but as great as he was, he was not as great as the least of those in the Kingdom of God.*

These words of Jesus regarding his cousin, John, deserve more spiritual thought. In those words Jesus was proclaiming a new and greater Kingdom—the Kingdom of God. But he was also sending another message to us.

All of us on earth are sinners. We are plagued with the stain of original sin. Throughout our life on earth we do not escape that sin. Our Lord was telling us that even though there was no greater person who lived on this earth, John too did not enter this earth free of that sin. But nevertheless our Lord told us no one on earth was greater than John. What exactly He meant is ours to contemplate. But in the eyes of Jesus, greatness of a man would surely be defined as one who most often was able to rise above the temptations to sin on this earth.

And yet through his words about John, our Lord gave us another message. Even though He proclaimed John as the greatest among men on earth, He also said he was not as great as the least of those who would be in the Kingdom of God. Jesus had not as yet been crucified for our sins when He spoke those words, but following his crucifixion He would open the Kingdom "when He descended into hell and on the third day rose again from the dead". This is the belief we Christians state when we recite the Nicene Creed.

Jesus was telling us that the least in that Kingdom would be greater than his beloved John. His words say so much about that Kingdom, which our human eyes have not seen and our human ears have not heard. If we live our lives as our Lord tells us to live it we can one day enter that Kingdom. When Jesus called John the greatest among those on earth He was also promising John a still greater place in his Kingdom. For John, who had offered his entire life to acceptance of sacrifice and suffering of life on earth, was yet to experience a greater life in the Kingdom provided by his Savior's death on the cross. It would be in Heaven that John would come face to face with perfect love.

Our Lord was to demonstrate his great love for all of us through the pain and suffering of his death on a cross. Through his words of greatness about John He was also giving us a message that by emulating the sacrifices and sufferings of John, we too can one day partake of the greatness of his Kingdom.

John's life was most assuredly a life dedicated to his father's words of preparing a way for the Lord. John accomplished that in a manner our Lord recognized as greater than any other man on earth.

Those words of greatness Jesus spoke of John are words all of us on earth should consider as to what "greatness" should mean for us. John eschewed all the material things of earth, even to wearing clothes of camel's hair and eating locust and wild honey. It was not the things of earth that made John great. It was his dedication and love of the Divine Man who would bring salvation to all of us that brought greatness to John.

It is that same dedication to the love of our Lord that brings greatness to each of us. As John demonstrated, that greatness does not come about because of our accomplishments on earth but rather what we accomplish in preparation for the Kingdom he promised us. Our suffering and sacrifices on behalf of Him and our fellow humans is the greatness of which our Lord spoke when He called John the greatest among men born of women. Such suffering and sacrifice is love. In John, He gave us the right role model

CHAPTER 4

THE APOSTLES

During his time on earth, Jesus selected a group of individuals who, after his death, would carry on the ministry He had begun during his time on earth. These Apostles were probably closer to Jesus during his public life on earth than anyone other than his mother.

Jesus did not select the chief priests of the Pharisees and Sadducees to be his Apostles. Rather he selected a group of ordinary, but very humble men. They were humble inasmuch as they would forsake their earthly positions and possessions to dedicate and sacrifice their lives to the service of our Lord. They would also endure great suffering and most would die for their faith.

Who were these men?

Simon Peter and Andrew—The first of the Apostles was St. Andrew. He was a follower of John the Baptist and an early believer that Jesus was the Messiah. He

George E Pfautsch

soon would introduce Jesus to his brother Simon. Andrew and Simon Peter were sons of Jonah. They were born in Bethsaida of Galilee on the east bank of the Sea of Galilee. Both were fisherman and are believed to have lived together in the town of Capernaum. Scripture tells us that Peter had a mother-in-law so we know Peter was married but are not certain about Andrew. Some historians believe he remained single. Both left a profitable fishing business to follow Jesus and become his early followers. They would sacrifice everything they owned.

James and John—These two Apostles were very close to Jesus. They were the sons of Zebedee and Salome. Their father, Zebedee, was a fairly prosperous fisherman and they were called to follow Jesus as they were mending their fishing nets with their father on Lake Genesareth. As was true of Peter and Andrew, they too were natives of the region of Galilee. They were nicknamed the "Sons of Thunder" by our Lord. Their closeness to Jesus was evident by the fact that they along with Peter were present at the Transfiguration and other significant events in the life of Jesus.

Philip and Bartholomew (Nathanael)—Shortly after (John 1-41 states the next day) Jesus chose Simon Peter and Andrew he went to Galilee and found Philip and told him, "Follow me". Philip was also from Bethsaida as were Peter and Andrew. Philip then found Nathanael and told him that they had found the Messiah from Nazareth. When Nathanael heard that Jesus was from Nazareth he would say, "Can anything good come from Nazareth?" When Nathanael approached Jesus our Lord would say, "Here is a true Israelite. There is no duplicity in him". In the course of their conversation Nathaneal would acknowledge Jesus as the Son of God and the King of Israel.

The Other Apostles—Thomas who was called Didymus was the Apostle who would be absent at a dinner when Jesus appeared to the other Apostles. Because of his doubts he earned the nickname, "Doubting Thomas". Matthew was the notorious tax collector, whose place with Jesus would be a matter of concern to the Pharisees. James the Less, was the son of Alphaeus of whom little is known. Judas who was also called Thaddeus is sometimes claimed to be the author of the Epistle of St. Jude but that is not a certainty. The eleventh Apostle was named Simon the Zealot or Canaanite and the twelfth was Judas Iscariot who would betray Jesus. After his betrayal and suicide Judas would be replaced by Matthias at about the time of Pentecost.

These were ordinary men with very ordinary positions in life. We do know four were fishermen and one was a publican and tax collector, but we know little about the backgrounds of the other Apostles. With his selection of these Apostles, Jesus demonstrated, as noted earlier, that He did not have to surround himself with the chief priests from the ranks of the Pharisees or Sadducees but, rather, with very ordinary people.

The life of Jesus and his Apostles can serve as a reminder to us that we are not called on to do extraordinary feats or perform in executive positions, but that we should go about our daily chores doing things as He would have us do them.

One of the important things to remember about the Apostles is that they gave up their earthly jobs and earthly possessions to become the first avid followers of our Lord. When he sent them forth to perform their ministries, He sent them forth with very little in the way of earthly possessions. They were expected to make and did make many sacrifices as his Apostles.

Jesus would demonstrate his great love for them and others through his Passion and Death for mankind's sins, but be also expected much from them.

He not only asked them to sacrifice their earthly possessions on his behalf but they would sacrifice their life because of their faith in Him.

St. Peter became the leader of the Christians once Jesus had ascended into Heaven. He designated Matthias to be the Apostle to replace Judas Iscariot. He was the first of the apostles to preach to the Gentiles and was the first to perform miracles. He was imprisoned by Herod Agrippa but was guided to freedom by an angel. Sacred Scripture says little of Peter after that escape, but tradition says he went to Rome and became its first Bishop and our first Pope. During the reign of Emperor Nero, Peter was crucified upside down at the foot of Vatican Hill. His whole life was a lesson in love of our Lord, even through great sacrifices and great suffering.

Our Lord also indicated via Peter that despite our human flaws, He loves us greatly. Peter claimed that he would never deny Christ but he did so three times before the cock crowed. Sometimes our suffering comes from the understanding that we are sinners and need his mercy and love. It may be no coincidence that our Lord asked Peter three times if he really loved Him. Despite his human flaws our Lord handpicked Peter to lead His Church.

Andrew, the brother of Peter, as already noted, was the first of the Apostles. Scripture tells us little of St. Andrew following the death of Jesus. He reportedly did some preaching in Scythia and Greece. We do not know for certain how he died but a long standing tradition notes he was crucified on a X shaped cross in Acaia. He, as his brother Peter, dedicated his life to our Lord, which demanded great sacrifices and also death on a cross.

James throughout the life of Jesus on earth was one of the Apostles who seemed to have a close relationship with our Savior. He along with Peter and his brother, John, were present when Jesus raised the daughter of Jairus from the dead. According to Scripture they were the three who were also present at the Transfiguration and during the agony of Jesus in the Garden of Gethsemane. Based on the "Acts of the Apostles" James was also the first of the apostles to be martyred. He was beheaded on the order of Herod Agrippa.

John, the younger brother of James, was also close to our Lord and many believe he was closer to our Lord on a personal basis than any of the other Apostles. At his Crucifixion, our Lord requested John to care for the Blessed Mother after his own death. It is reported that he escaped martyrdom during the reign of Emperor Domitian while he was in Rome, by miraculously emerging unscathed from a large kettle of boiling oil. He was subsequently exiled to the island of Patmos. He is believed to be the writer of the fourth gospel and some believe is also the author of Revelations, but that is much debated. He spent many years in Ephesus which is where the Blessed Mother also spent many of her final years on earth. It is believed that John is the only Apostle, who escaped martyrdom.

All the remaining Apostles who preached the Word of God and dedicated their lives to disseminating the Good News were also martyred. Philip, as was true of Peter, is believed to have been crucified upside down during the reign of Emperor Domitian. Not much is known of the works of Bartholomew. It is believed that he preached in India and also greater Armenia. It was in Armenia, where traditions has it that he was beaten and beheaded.

The remaining Apostles are also believed to have been martyred. The reason for their martyrdom resulted from bringing the Word of God to many in environments, which were hostile toward Christianity.

All of the Apostles sacrificed worldly possessions to do the bidding of our Lord. All were willing to experience hardships and disavow material things for that bidding and all, except John, gave their lives as martyrs in that pursuit. The Apostles truly were role models in how to learn greater love through suffering and sacrifice

CHAPTER 5

SAINT PAUL

Although not one of the twelve Apostles, Saint Paul did much to spread Christianity in the early years of the Church. It was primarily St. Paul who brought Christianity to the Gentiles. It would not be an exaggeration to refer to him as the senior marketing vice-president for Jesus. His would be a life that was filled with a great deal of suffering and sacrifice on behalf of our Lord. Through his writings and the Acts of the Apostles we would learn much of this saint and his love of Christ.

But his early years would not be ones that were dedicated to Christianity. It is believed that Saint Paul was born sometime around the year 10 AD. He was born in Tarsus to Jewish parents from the tribe of Benjamin. Being born in Tarsus made him a citizen of Rome. He would study in Jerusalem under the famous Jewish Rabbi, Gamaliel. He would become a strict Pharisee. By trade he was a tentmaker.

As a Pharisee, he also became a persecutor of the early Christians. He was a spectator when St. Stephen was stoned to death. Tradition does not indicate that he was a participant in the stoning.

St. Paul's life would take a dramatic turn not too long after the Crucifixion of Jesus. It occurred one day when he was on his way to Damascus to arrest some Christians and bring them back to Jerusalem in chains. Chapter 9 of the Acts tell us of his conversion during his journey. *As he was nearing Damascus, a light from the sky suddenly flashed around him. He fell to the ground and heard a voice saying to him, "Saul, Saul, why are you persecuting me?" He said, "Who are you, sir?" The reply came, "I am Jesus, whom you are persecuting. Now get up and you will be told what you must do." The men who were traveling with him stood speechless, for they heard the voice but could see no one. Saul got up from the ground, but when he opened his eyes he could see nothing so they led him by the hand and brought him to Damascus. For three days he was unable to see, and he neither ate nor drank.*

Ananias, a disciple, lived in Damascus and Jesus appeared to him in a vision. He asked Ananias to visit Saul and lay his hands on Saul so he would regain his sight. Ananias was reluctant, because he had heard of Saul and his persecution of Christians. But Jesus assured him that He had chosen Saul (Paul) to carry Christianity to many parts of the world. Ananias did as the Lord requested and after Paul regained his sight he was baptized. Thus began the journey of one of, if not, the greatest evangelists in the history of the Church. It is interesting that Jesus would pick Paul who until his conversion had been anything but a champion of Christianity.

St. Paul would toil relentlessly to spread the Gospel. He would sacrifice much and suffer a great deal in that pursuit. We will review some of those tribulations. After his conversion Paul is believed to have spent three years in Arabia, after which he would return to Damascus. He would encounter resistance to his preaching from the Jews. Such resistance would continue throughout his life and throughout his many travels.

He was forced to flee the region of Damascus. After some time preaching in the region, the Jews conspired to kill him, but the Acts of the Apostles tells us that St. Paul learned of their plot. The Acts go on to tell us that he was able to escape because his disciples would lower him in a basket through an opening in a wall.

From the region of Damascus, Paul would return to Jerusalem. Initially the other disciples were "afraid" of Paul and did not believe him to be a disciple. But Barnabas, another follower of Jesus, and also a student of Gamaliel, took Paul under his wing. Once the other disciples heard and understood the story of his conversion he was accepted by them and moved about Jerusalem proclaiming the Good News of our Lord. Once again his life was threatened and this time it was by the Hellenists. When the disciples heard of this they took him to Caesarea and sent him to Tarsus. On these early missionary journeys he was accompanied by Barnabas.

With the many travel modes available today, we do not think too much of the many miles that Paul travelled to spread the word of the Lord. But in Paul's time, these journeys could be lengthy and hazardous. Paul seemed not to let these constant risks stand in his way. His fervent faith and his love of our Lord, would overcome many obstacles.

When in Philippi, he would be imprisoned along with Silas but both would miraculously escape.

In Chapter 16 of the Acts of the Apostles we are told of the imprisonment, beatings, and the escape of Paul from Philippi.

Paul would visit many places spreading the word of God. They included Thessalonica, Beroea, Antioch, Corinth and others. His letters to many of his followers became a part of Holy Scripture.

He spent two years teaching and preaching in Ephesus, where St. John and the mother of Jesus also spent much time. It seems likely that their paths would have crossed. We are left to ponder if they may have had frequent visits together to discuss the great wonders of our Lord. Here again, we have the opportunity for meditation.

St. Paul was also driven from Ephesus. This time it was not for reasons of what he was teaching but because he was hurting the business of the silversmiths. These silversmiths made a livelihood selling statues and other icons of Diana, the pagan goddess. They feared that Paul's teaching would hurt their trade and their protestations forced him to leave.

Sometime later, Paul would return to Jerusalem and would again be arrested. He not only preached to his fellow Jews but also to Gentiles. It was for bringing the Good News to the Gentiles that he was attacked and put under the protective custody of Roman soldiers. His life was threatened and the Roman captain decided to send him to the Governor of Caesarea who was then Felix. He was held there for a couple of years while his trial was delayed. When Festus succeeded Felix, his trial began. At that point Paul demanded that he as a Roman citizen be tried in Rome and that demand was granted.

On his way to Rome, Paul would undergo another severe trial in his life. During his travels, he was shipwrecked near the island of Malta. He survived and eventually made it to Rome. In Rome he remained under house arrest for two more years. Up to that point in his life much of the biographical information regarding St. Paul is contained in the Acts of the Apostles.

After being imprisoned for some time it is believed that he went to Spain. Based on his letters he also revisited Ephesus and other places where he had established churches earlier. It is also believed that following his imprisonment in Rome he was again imprisoned somewhere in what is now Turkey and again sent to Rome.

There are some who believe that he and St. Peter were executed on the same day in Rome, during a period when Christians were being persecuted by the Emperor Nero, but others believe that is unlikely. It is uncertain when St. Paul died but Christian tradition indicates that his execution was accomplished around the year 67 by beheading.

In addition to spreading the word of God far and wide, St. Paul was also a Christian writer. He is the patron saint of writers. His writings became a significant and substantial part of the New Testament. By both word and pen he was indeed a great marketing executive for our Lord.

Following his conversion, he displayed an unbelievable fervent faith and a great love of our Lord. His writings are sometimes lengthy one sentence paragraphs. But his love of Christ is evident through those writings. He writes eloquently of the soul and of the importance of love. His life was one of sacrifice and suffering and he finally laid down his life for his faith.

We end this chapter with two of my favorite passages from the writing of St. Paul. In his letter to the Galatians St. Paul warns us of the dangers of desiring things of the flesh. But he goes on to describe the beautiful characteristics of our soul—*In contrast, the fruit of the Spirit is love, joy, peace, patience, kindness, generosity, faithfulness, gentleness, self-control.* What a beautiful world this would be if each minute of every day, each human being would be directed by those traits. It is those traits that come from the soul, that special creation of God.

In his letter to the Corinthians he would elaborate even more on the importance of love.

If I speak in human and angelic tongues but do not have love, I am a resounding gong or a clashing cymbal. And if I have the gift of prophecy and comprehend all mysteries and all knowledge: and if I have all faith so as to move mountains but do not have love, I am nothing. If I give away everything I own, and if I hand my body over so that I may boast but do not have love I gain nothing.

Love is patient, love is kind. It is not jealous, it is not pompous, it is not inflated, it is not rude, it does not seek its own interests, it is not quick-tempered, it does not brood over injury, it does not rejoice over wrongdoing but rejoices with the truth. It bears all things, believes all things, hopes all things, endures all things.

Love never fails.

St. Paul sacrificed his life. St. Paul endured much suffering. St. Paul loved his God in all ways and through all things

CHAPTER 6

THE HOLY INNOCENTS, ST. STEPHEN AND MARTYRDOM

Throughout the history of the Church many have given their life for their faith. The history of Christian martyrdom began shortly after the birth of our Lord. We should spend a moment on those considered the very first of martyrs, the Holy Innocents. The massacre of the Innocents occurred during the reign of the King of Judea, Herod the Great. The story of the Innocents is provided in the 2nd Chapter of Matthew.

And having been warned in a dream not to return to Herod, they (the Magi) departed for their country by another way.

When they departed, behold, the angel of the Lord appeared to Joseph in a dream and said, "Rise, take the child and his mother, flee to Egypt, and stay there until I tell you. Herod is going to search for the child to destroy him. Joseph rose and took the child and his mother by night and departed for Egypt. He stayed there until the death of Herod, that what the Lord had said through the prophet might be fulfilled, "Out of Egypt I called my son."

When Herod realized that he had been deceived by the magi, be became furious. He ordered the massacre of all the boys in Bethlehem and its vicinity, two years old and under, in accordance with the time he had ascertained from the magi. Then was fulfilled what had been said through Jeremiah, the prophet: "A voice was heard in Ramah, sobbing and loud lamentation; Rachel weeping for her children, and she would not be consoled, since they were no more."

History has not provided the number of infant boys that were killed. The Church celebrates the Feast Day of the Holy Innocents on December 28 and the gospel reading for that day is much of the 2nd Chapter of St. Matthew noted above. On that day the celebrant of the Mass wears the traditional red vestments for martyrs.

The Feast of Holy Innocents should serve as a reminder that the lives of infants, including the preborn are precious to our Lord. He endowed all of them with an immortal soul. In the world we live in today, infanticide through abortions, is far, far too widespread and is unfortunately condoned by too many, including those in government.

Even though these little children may not have understood the meaning of faith, they nevertheless sacrificed their lives for our Lord.

It would not be long after the massacre of the Holy Innocents that individuals would sacrifice their lives for our Lord. On the day after Christmas, and two days before the feast of the Holy Innocents, the Church celebrates the Feast Day of St. Stephen, the first individual martyr of the Church.

In Chapter 6 of the Acts of the Apostles we are told that Stephen was chosen as one of the "seven reputable men" of the Hellenic Jewish community by the Apostles to take care of the secular needs of that community. It is believed that Stephen was a wise and learned Jewish man who may have been educated in Alexandria. One can assume that Stephen was the leader of the seven men selected by the Apostles.

Stephen would engage many of the Jewish leaders in debate but the Acts of the Apostles states—"they could not withstand the wisdom and the spirit with which he spoke".

Stephen's discourses are covered in Chapter 7 of the Acts of the Apostles. His concluding words from the discourse are worth noting—*You stiff-necked people, uncircumcised in heart and ears, you always oppose the holy Spirit: you are just like your ancestors. Which of the prophets did your ancestors not persecute? They put to death those who foretold the coming of the righteous one, whose betrayers and murderers you have now*

George E Pfautsch

become. You received the law as transmitted by angels but you did not observe it."

After these words Stephen saw a vision; "the heavens opened and the Son of Man standing at the right hand of God". Stephen was then led out of the city and stoned to death. In attendance to the stoning was St. Paul shortly before his conversion.

As many after him, St. Stephen would die because of his fervent faith and love of our Lord and Savior. Martyrs who followed his example would be numerous throughout the history of the past 2,000 years.

We could continue on with many of those who gave their lives for their faith. It has been an unfortunate part of history that people have had to give their life, purely for their love of a merciful, kind and just God. Since the time of Jesus we have many examples of those who have died for their faith.

Maybe the word unfortunate is a word that should not be used to define martyrdom. But for those of us on earth, who lack the spiritual wisdom needed to understand fully the love of God of those in his Kingdom it is thought of in that manner. It may be more fitting that a martyr be viewed as one who has demonstrated great love of God.

Nevertheless, we look upon martyrdom as a terrible punishment for faith and find it hard to understand why people must suffer horrible deaths, as many martyrs did.

Not as much is written about the great love involved in the suffering of these martyrs as is written about the sacrifice and suffering involved. Why would someone be willing to lay down their life for their belief? One of the answers to that question can be found in our Lord's passion and death. He was willing to demonstrate his great love for all of us by dying for our sins. He died so we might gain eternal salvation, which is the ultimate happiness for those on earth.

Our Lord also told us that greater love cannot be demonstrated than the willingness to lay down one's life for another.

That type of love is not easy to define. Love of God transcends all other love. As we become more guided by spiritual wisdom we also grow in love of our Lord. As we grow the love of our Lord, it becomes the uppermost value in our life.

The love of God is difficult to define because faith too is difficult to define. Faith is necessary to grow our love of God and neighbor. It is from faith that we know Him and increase our love of Him. It is also through the love of God that we love our neighbor as our self.

Love of God includes a willingness to endure sacrifices and suffering. The greater the love the greater the willingness to endure sacrifice and suffering. As we love God more and our neighbor more, we begin to understand better that our life belongs to Him and others as much as it belongs to us.

When a human being loves God with the greatest fervor of faith possible on this earth, that human being begins to believe more and more that any sacrifice or suffering can be endured for the love of Him who loved us so much that He was willing to die for each and every one of us. He asks no more of us than He asked of Himself.

Through this and prior chapters we have looked at Jesus, Mary and others who lived at or near the time of Christ on earth. But we need not have lived in that era to experience greater love through sacrifice and suffering.

Throughout the history of the Church there have been many who have sacrificed their lives for love of Him. There have also been some saints and others who have endured the stigmata, or five wounds of Christ. They include St. Francis of Assisi, St. Catherine of Siena, St. Faustina Kowalska, St. Padre Pio and many others. These saints shared a special suffering and love with our Lord, inasmuch as they were asked to share some of the pain He suffered for us.

We will now turn to more modern times, and look at those who more recently have also experienced greater love of God and neighbor through sacrifice and suffering.

CHAPTER 7

THE DISABLED AND AGED

In the world we live in today, much sacrifice and suffering exists. Just as it was at the time of Jesus such sacrifice and suffering can also be turned to greater love.

Many on earth today are mentally and physically challenged. We have those among us who have had birth defects. We have those who have been injured. We have veterans who have fought in wars and have been harmed while serving their country and fellow citizens.

Let us begin with children. There are many children who have either mental or physical disabilities. We need not list them all because that alone would entail looking at tens if not hundreds of causes of different types of child disabilities.

Many families have members who are mentally or physically disabled. My family was no exception and since I lived with that it is the example I can best describe.

When he was a teenager, my younger brother, Johnny, was diagnosed as an adolescent schizophrenic. I remember being with my father and older brother on the day the doctor gave us that opinion. At that point Johnny had just turned seventeen and I was a newlywed. We had already known that our brother was mentally challenged but were not exactly sure of the cause.

His illness not only caused him great suffering but also caused many heartbreaks for my parents and the rest of the family. For the rest of his life he was loved by all of us in a special way, even though sacrifice accompanied that love. Johnny never married and lived with my parents until their deaths. Johnny would then live by himself under the watchful eye and care of our oldest brother and the rest of the family. In his final years on earth he also lived with our youngest brother, who in his youth experienced life living with an older impaired brother.

In addition to his mental disease, Johnny became a paraplegic in the final months of his life following a fall. He died at a rather young age. I remember well the words our oldest brother wrote for his eulogy. "All of us on earth need someone to care for—Johnny was our someone".

I cannot improve on those words. Johnny suffered a great deal in life on earth. He in turn was greatly loved by those of us who were close to him and we pray that he now is loved in Heaven for the sacrifice and suffering he experienced in this world.

Johnny's story can be repeated by many other families who have members that are either mentally or physically disabled. It can create a special and loving bond for them and those who love them.

But that greater love does not end with their life on earth. We do not know and probably don't understand very well why our Lord permits such hardships for so many here on earth. But we also do not understand the place He may have prepared for them in his eternal Kingdom. During his time on earth He demonstrated great compassion for those who were disabled. We can be reasonably assured that He will also continue to demonstrate great compassion for those who have been disabled since his time on earth.

It is an unfortunate reality that in the world today too many people see only the hardship side of those with mental and physical handicaps. Too frequently a purely secular humanistic view is taken for those who are disabled. With modern technology many of those disabilities can now be detected before birth and too many women are being advised to abort such children. The spiritual aspect of those type decisions are often ignored in making the decisions. Because of the large number of abortions in this world a separate chapter will be devoted to aborted infants.

In addition to those born with disabilities, we also have those who have become disabled through accidents and wars. It is especially appropriate to address our veterans who have been wounded in battle.

Our Lord stated that there was no greater love than to lay down one's life for his fellow man. By the mere fact that our servicemen and servicewomen are in the military indicates their willingness to lay down their life. Those killed in action have fulfilled that act of love of which our Lord speaks. Those who are wounded in action also have been willing to do that and many of them spend the remainder of their lives enduring the pain incurred through their willingness to lay down their lives so others may live.

Those who have been willing to lay down their lives so others may live in freedom deserve the admiration of those for whom they have sacrificed and suffered. Through the history of this universe there have been many wars that have been waged so some ruthless people might stay in power. But there are also very many who have fought so others may have the inalienable right of liberty bestowed on them by a gracious God who gives humans that right.

There is another group of people who are subjected to pain and suffering. As people in this nation live longer we have more senior citizens among us. The aged have more health issues than their younger counterparts, but they also have great spiritual opportunities. Growing spiritual wisdom can be a part of the aging process and they have many opportunities to increase their love of God through the pain, suffering and sacrifices that aging brings.

Cancer, diabetes, hearing impairment, sight impairment, and other impairments of bodily functions often accompany aging. But these disabling afflictions can be offered up to our Lord as sacrifices incurred so we might have a greater love of Him. When these afflictions occur, the aged can reflect and meditate on He who died on the cross so we might have eternal happiness with Him. When we reflect and remember that He endured that great suffering because He loved us, then we can more easily turn our sufferings into a greater love of Him.

By remembering his pain and death on the Cross, we are better able to carry our cross during our periods of suffering on earth. We can offer these sufferings to Him so that we and others for whom we offer them may have a greater closeness and understanding of what He endured for our sins and for the love of us.

The elderly suffer not only from a greater amount of physical impairments but also from greater mental impairments. With advancing age comes the greater likelihood of dementia or Alzheimer's disease. Most of us view these as terrible afflictions of the aged when they occur.

But these afflictions of our earthly mind, may also be reason to examine more closely their spiritual potential. When we die the brain ceases all functioning and yet we of faith know that the soul will continue to live through all eternity following our bodily death.

The soul is the vessel of spirituality. We do not know for sure that upon death, if the soul will be immediately enlightened or how that enlightenment takes place. Our time on earth may be a gradual process of preparing our soul for Heaven, and it may be that process continues after death. We don't know. It is worth contemplation.

Such contemplation may more fully help us understand that preparing our soul for Heaven is a process that must be an ongoing process on earth. It is our purpose on earth to know, love and serve God and thereby gain Heaven. It is also true that we do not know the time or the place that we will depart this earth so we must always be prepared for that eventuality.

Those who we consider to be suffering greatly from dementia or Alzheimer's may merely be a step closer to their final destiny in life hereafter. If souls after death have the function to reason and comprehend then such souls may also have that function while the body is suffering from dementia or Alzheimer's. We should not assume that because the human brain is impaired that the immortal soul is likewise impaired.

In doing some research for an earlier book and also for this book, I interviewed a number of people who worked with or were associated with those suffering from dementia or Alzheimer's.

A great majority of them stated that such "mentally impaired" elderly people maintained their understanding of prayer, albeit some in a more simple form. But maybe, just maybe, that simplicity is a reflection of an untroubled soul, that is less encumbered by a sinful body. If such a soul is in a state of grace, it may already be in a greater state of those attributes St. Paul attributed to the soul—love, joy, peace, patience, kindness, generosity, faithfulness, gentleness, and self-control.

There may also be those suffering from dementia or Alzheimer's whose souls are not as yet prepared for entry to Heaven. For those of us who love and care for them, it may be well to recite simple prayers with them. Our Lord made it known to Saint Maria Faustina Kowalska, that those on their deathbed who sincerely recited the chaplet of "Divine Mercy" would be treated favorably at their judgment.

In our Lord's appearance to Saint Faustina, he spoke these words to her (1541 in her Dairy).

My daughter, encourage souls to say the chaplet which I have given you. It pleases Me to grant everything they ask of Me by saying the chaplet. When hardened sinners say it, I will fill their souls with peace, and the hour of their death will be a happy one.

Write this for the benefit of distressed souls: when a soul sees and realizes the gravity of its sins, when the whole abyss of the misery into which it immersed itself is displayed before its eyes, let it not despair . . . these souls have a right of priority to My compassionate Heart, they have first access to My mercy. Tell them that no soul that has called upon My mercy has been disappointed or brought to shame.

Write this that when they say this chaplet in the presence of the dying, I will stand between My Father and the dying person, not as the just Judge but as the merciful Savior.

We may think that those afflicted with dementia or Alzheimer's may not understand the beautiful words of the chaplet, but that may not be the will of our Lord. The story of the Prodigal Son tells us that there would and should be joy when a lost sheep is saved. We should assume that to also be true of those aged who are mentally impaired. Their soul may understand the words of the chaplet far beyond the assumptions we may make.

Only the Lord knows his plans for those who suffer from dementia or Alzheimer's but those of us on earth should not assume that their ability to fill their spiritual vessel has ended with their afflictions. Their pain and suffering may be a period of greater preparation for their eternity with Him.

The Divine Mercy chaplet is a wonderful prayer for all of us to pray each day for those who will depart earth on the day we pray it. Such a day may also be our last day on earth.

There is much pain and suffering that we encounter in our own life and in the lives of others during our time on earth. During such times we are able to strengthen our love for Him who endured even greater suffering and death for each of us.

CHAPTER 8

THE SOULS OF ABORTED INFANTS

In the world we live in today, it is a sad truth that there are many in power who do not believe in the sanctity of all lives. Some in the government of our own country espouse the pro-choice position which gives a higher priority for women to choose an abortion, than it gives to the life of a child in the womb. It is a viewpoint that is taken in too many nations in the world by far too many people in those nations.

It seems not to matter to many who take the pro-choice position that their claims of such a position is a contradiction to the position that they are Christian believers. Most Christian religions believe that a human body is endowed by our Creator with an immortal soul at conception. If we kill that human body, we do not permit that soul to live with the body throughout a life that otherwise may have been dedicated to knowing, loving and serving his/

her Creator. It is hypocritical to say I can be a good Christian and also be pro-choice. Spiritual wisdom is non-existent in making such a claim. One should not believe that it is a good Christian position to accept the existence of the 5th Commandment while also accepting the killing of a child that is endowed with an immortal soul.

It is not a purpose of this book to castigate those who are pro-choice. As the title indicates my purpose is to speak of the ways we can show a greater love to our God and our neighbor. If we wish to have a greater love of Christ then we must also have an increasing love of what He teaches (Christianity). Christianity also teaches us to love our neighbor as our self. Our neighbor includes the infant who is to be aborted. As Christians we should therefore ask our self—Do we wish that we would have been aborted?

But let us move on to viewing the soul of the aborted infant as our Lord may view that soul. As noted earlier, we believe that God breathes an immortal soul into the human body at the moment of conception. That soul is made in his image and likeness and as with all other immortal souls, it shares a special place in his Creation. God who so loved mankind that He died on the Cross so souls might have eternal life, is not a God who abandons souls. He could not do more than He did to show his love for the souls of all mankind.

Who is there to love the soul of the aborted infant? This infant has been abandoned by its mother and father. That special bond between a mother and child will not exist for the aborted infant. It will not know the love of other humans. Its soul will return to its Creator without that love of others on earth. But it is my belief that the immortal soul of abandoned infants will have a special place in the eyes of our Creator. He loved his Creation and he had a special love for the children he created. He would not be the kind and loving God that we who are believers, know Him to be, if aborted souls were not special to Him.

It is not difficult for us to believe that our Lord will compensate for the love the souls of these tiny infants will not experience on earth. He frequently mentioned the need to love and care for the poor and also children. We on earth do not understand how our soul will relate to our Maker after death. It is also beyond our knowledge to understand how our Lord will treat the souls of the abandoned and aborted infant. But He who died for us because of his great love for us, will not be among those who abandon these infants. As He told Jeremiah, "Before you were in your mother's womb, I knew you". He knows and loves each soul He created and that most assuredly extends to the soul of the aborted infant.

Will He treat them as the other souls who experience life on earth? We don't know but it is worth pondering. Will they be treated as other baptized souls who die in infancy? We don't know but we can assume the aborted soul has received the Baptism of blood. Therefore, would our Lord treat these abandoned souls any less than he would treat a soul of another infant who has already been born but who also dies in infancy? The Just Judge is also our compassionate and merciful Lord and Redeemer.

As we contemplate the souls of these abandoned infants, we should be led to prayer for them. We should also be led to pray for those mothers who may be contemplating abortion. We should pray for the father who abandons the woman who aborts his child. They need our prayers. In a world that is becoming ever more humanistic and less faithful, these souls need our prayers.

Life is a spiritual warfare and thus it has been since Creation. Good and evil have always existed. In the 20th and 21st centuries we have permitted abortions to be the barbarism of the modern era. We often look repulsively at the cruel methods that earlier civilizations have used to murder others within their society. We should be similarly repulsed by the killing of defenseless and innocent preborn human beings.

As previously noted, there are many associated with abortions who need our prayers. It is my hope that all readers of this book will pray that all of us on earth may increase our understanding of the sanctity of life.

But we also know there is a kind and merciful Savior. He died on the Cross because He loved us.

Even though the souls of the aborted preborn have been deprived of the love of fellow humans in this world, we can rest assured that our Lord's love extends to the souls of the aborted infants.

CHAPTER 9

THE POOR OF THE WORLD

One thing our Lord left no doubt about is his sentiment for the poor of the world. Even before He took on the nature of man, the Old Testament made clear that sins against children and widows were offenses that cried out to Heaven. In the New Testament our Lord frequently spoke of his compassion for the poor and demonstrated his love of the poor through numerous miracles that aided the poor.

Sacred Scripture defines the poor in a couple of ways. There are those who are poor in material things and there are also those who are poor in spirit. Our Lord spoke kindly of both.

It is an unfortunate truth, that through much of the history of mankind, those in power have not done a good job of providing a better world for the poor in their countries. Serfdom, slavery, caste systems and just plain neglect are too great a part of history.

Many of those in power have often claimed that more should be done for the poor, but in turn do little to aid them. That accusation leads to the issue of what it is that can best be done for the poor.

Certainly one thing that can be done is to have a government that recognizes the inalienable rights God gave to all people. Those rights were very well set forth by the founding fathers of this country. It is important to recognize that Our Creator granted the inalienable rights of life, liberty and the pursuit of happiness to all human beings. It is also important that governments recognize that all human beings are created equal. By recognizing and granting these rights governments do not stand opposed to the will of God who gave these rights to all people.

By recognizing that all humans are created equal and are granted inalienable rights, governments provide an equal opportunity to all people. In doing that, governments take an important first step in aiding the poor and government's first responsibility should be that of caring for all its citizens. Thereby, governments also embrace the Lord's command that we love one another as he loved us.

Our Lord must have understood that too many governments and too many others stand in the way of aiding the poor. In the old Testament, He warned those who harmed widows and children (the poor) that such sins were sins which cried out to Heaven. He encouraged all of us to show our love for those who cannot always care for themselves and He certainly expressed his own love for them.

There are many other ways to help and love the poor. Missions exist in poor countries that can be supported, hospitals and schools can be helped, and crises centers for poor children exist that need our help. There are many ways all of us can be helpful to those who need such help.

It is unfortunate that there are nations and organizations that do not help the poor despite their intent to do so. In the 19th century, Karl Marx, the German philosopher and economist, popularized the slogan, "From each according to his ability, to each according to his need".

For those who believe all people are created equal that is a slogan that would seem to have a great deal of merit. It was used frequently by those who wished to advance the socialist movement.

There is one very major problem with the slogan and socialist governments. Who is in charge and can they be trusted? The problem with putting all property in the hands of government and having government determine the distribution of wealth is that such governments have an extraordinary amount of power. Power tends to corrupt and that has been the problem with such governments. Power is maintained at the top echelons of government and the people become subjected and subservient to such governments. The overriding problem with the

Marx slogan is that it overlooks the dangers of having power vested in a few hands and that little power is placed in the hands of the many.

The people of our nation are fortunate that the founding fathers understood such dangers and recognized that it was our Creator who endowed people with the inalienable rights to life, liberty and the pursuit of happiness. It is not an easy role for governments to maintain a governance that benefits its entire population including the poor.

It is often easier to recognize the needs of the poor who are lacking in material needs, than it is to recognize other forms of poorness. Many times it is not so easy to recognize the needs of those who are mentally poor. We too often blame someone's inability to address their own needs because they are addicted to alcohol or drugs. We too often blame laziness for those who cannot find employment. In truth we do not know what may drive such people to their problems and the Lord made it clear that we too should love all others as he loved us. He did not make exceptions.

The Lord made it clear that we should demonstrate our love to those who are poor due to living in nations where governments may impede their ability to help themselves. He also made it clear to help those who are mentally or physically disabled.

But our Lord in his love also noted very specifically that "the poor in spirit" are blessed. Therein is a great challenge and opportunity for all of us to demonstrate our love for Him.

Who is included among "the poor in spirit". Certainly a basic necessity to be included is to have the virtue of humility. It is through humility that we strengthen our faith. It is through humility that we can better love our Lord with all strength of mind. It is through humility that we recognize we are poor and futile human beings and that it is only our Lord who saves us through his death on the cross.

It does not require one to be poor in material things to be poor in spirit. Being poor in spirit does not mean we must ignore the talents He gave us. Being poor in spirit does not mean that we must degrade ourselves.

Having said the above, it is an unfortunate truth that an excessive amount of material things seems to lead to a loss of humility and a loss of the belief that only through his mercy do we gain the ability to gain eternal happiness.

It is through the deepest form of humility that we become poorer in spirit. Being poor in spirit encompasses an honest evaluation of ourselves, which includes the recognition that we are sinners and that He grants us mercy. It is an understanding that we are indeed poor in our own abilities to merit our own salvation and thus recognizing that we are in dire need of his mercy.

As just noted, being poor in spirit must include the recognition that we need his mercy. That recognition does not demand that we do not use our talents or live in poverty. That recognition also does not mean we must spend every day with an inferiority complex. We can achieve great things here on earth and still be "poor in spirit". When we understand each and every day that it is He who gave us our talents and our desire to work than there is nothing wrong with using those talents and those desires for the good of others and our self.

God truly loved the poor. He loved and wanted us to love those who need material things which they cannot obtain for themselves. That does not mean that the poor should not make an effort to help themselves, but it does mean that we should help those who cannot help themselves.

God also loves the "poor in spirit" because they also love Him greatly. It is the love that emanates from the knowledge that He is our merciful God and without his great mercy and love we are helpless to gain eternal salvation. It must begin with great humility.

Earlier in this chapter we noted the slogan of Karl Marx and the failures of the socialist movement. It is not only governments, but also organizations that fail in efforts to help the poor.

The Catechism of the Catholic Church, 1883 states the following—*Socialization also presents dangers. Excessive intervention by the state can threaten personal freedom and initiative. The teaching of the Church has elaborated the principle of "subsidiarity", according to which a community of a higher order should not interfere in the internal life of a community of a lower order, depriving the latter of its functions, but rather should support it in case of need and help to co-ordinate its activity with the activities of the rest of society, always with a view to the common good.*

In 1884, it goes on to say—God has not willed to reserve to himself all exercise of power. He entrusts to every creature the functions it is capable of performing, according to the capacities of its own nature. This mode of governance ought to be followed in social life. The way God acts in governing the world, which bears witness to such great regard for human freedom, should inspire the wisdom of those who govern human communities. They should behave as ministers of divine providence.

Once again, as was true with the slogan of Karl Marx, the words are good and the ideals are morally correct. The problem is that we human beings who should behave as ministers of divine providence too often fail to do so. We are sinners and that does not exclude those who serve as ministers of divine providence. Even within the Church there have been failures and one such example will be explored in the next chapter. Subsidiarity needs more application within Church organizations, when such organizations are dealing with issues not directly related to faith and moral teaching

CHAPTER 10

THE CASE OF THE POOR CHILDREN IN HONDURAS

Our life on earth is a life of spiritual warfare. There are no better words to explain that warfare than were written by St. Paul in his letter to the Romans: *What I do, I do not understand, for I do not do what I want, but I do what I hate. Now if I do what I do not want, I concur that the law is good. So now it is no longer I who do it, but sin that dwells within me, that is my flesh. The willing is at hand, but doing the good is not.*

Humans struggle to do the right faith-based moral thing, because the flesh often interferes. Political parties in our country debate endlessly the path that best serves the poor. If those parties based their judgments on the teachings of our Lord, such debates could be short-lived. But they often depart from our Lord's teachings and pursue the path dictated by their own secular-based moral beliefs. Politicians are not the only ones who frequently take the wrong path.

This chapter will address a case where poor children were the victims of a case that involved people within the Church who could and should have done more to help them.

In the readings of the Mass on the day this chapter was first begun, both the first reading and the gospel informed us of the importance of faith. The first reading today was from St. Paul's letter to the Galatians and states the following: *Before faith came, we were held in custody under the law, confined for the faith that was to be revealed. Consequently, the law was our disciplinarian for Christ, that we might be justified by faith. But now that faith has come, we are no longer under a disciplinarian. For through faith you are children of God in Christ Jesus . . . There is neither Jew nor Greek, there is neither slave nor free person, there is not male or female: for you are all one in Christ Jesus.*

These words clearly tell us that it is our faith in Jesus that must be the path we follow. When we, the faithful, can discern the path to take from that which Jesus taught us, then we can be assured we have taken the right path.

In today's gospel from Luke, Jesus made that even more clear: *While Jesus was speaking, a woman from the crowd called out and said to him, "Blessed is the womb that carried you and the breasts at which you nursed." He replied, "Rather, blessed are those who hear the word of God and observe it."*

I do not think Jesus could have made it more clear that the words of God provide for each of us the right path to follow.

So what do all the above words mean as they relate to the poor? Because of the spiritual warfare first noted in this chapter, it is easy for us to think that the laws of our nation, state or even our religion must always be followed. Unfortunately there are times that such laws or their application can conflict with the words Jesus taught us.

Some time ago I wrote a book titled, "A Case of Modern Day Pharisees". It was a book that dealt with poor children in Honduras and how an excessive application of the laws and rules of a religious Order caused many poor children in Honduras to be deprived of a better life and hence were a violation of the teachings of our Lord to help the poor.

The essence of that book was captured in an article written by me in 2010 and subsequently published in the "Catholic Voice", a diocesan newspaper. It is reprinted below:

QUESTIONABLE APPLICATION OF BISHOPS' STANDARDS HARMING POOR

In light of numerous cases, it is understandable that the United States Conference of Catholic Bishops (USCCB) would insist on stringent standards to provide protection against the abuse of minors. But sometimes a questionable application of standards can have unintended harmful effects. That is the situation in a case that is now harming the poor, especially children, in Honduras and the Dominican Republic.

Forty years ago a humble missionary, Father Emil Cook, went to Honduras. As he saw firsthand the terrible conditions of the poor, especially children, he became a one person crusader to do something. During the forty years he formed an organization, APUFRAM, to carry out his vision of aiding others. APUFRAM (Spanish acronym for Association of Franciscan Boys' Towns and Girls' Towns) would operate not only in Honduras but also the Dominican Republic and Liberia.

The APUFRAM organization, comprised of people who had once been helped by Father Emil, became a missionary organization to help others around the world.

In early 2009, the good work of APUFRAM was jolted by the news of an alleged sexual abuse of a young woman in Liberia by one of the APUFRAM lay missionaries from Honduras. The incident was reported to Mission Honduras International (MHI), the US funding arm for APUFRAM. MHI suspended funding for APUFRAM and reported the incident to the Conventual Franciscan Order in the United States. Father Emil, who made annual fundraising trips to the United States, is a member of this Order.

By late 2009, because of additional alleged abuse cases made by MHI, the Conventual Franciscan Order decided to launch an investigation. Consequently, in attempting *to comply with their own rules and the Bishops' standards on child protection, the US Franciscans have advised all US Bishops that fundraising activities by Father Emil, APUFRAM and APUFRAM International (a new US group formed to provide financial support), both of which are secular organizations, were not acceptable in the United States. In addition, Father Emil was ordered to cut his ties with APUFRAM, while the investigation is ongoing, even though he is not accused of any personal sexual abuse. Father Emil claims, that other than the case in Liberia, which has been investigated and now made public, he has never been aware of any cases of child abuse within the APUFRAM organization.*

In October, 2009, in a joint letter distributed by MHI and APUFRAM, Father Emil apologized for any errors he and the APUFRAM Board made in the handling of the abuse case in Liberia, and in early 2010 the APUFRAM organization implemented a new and improved child protection plan. But, to date, the restrictions on funding have not been removed and the investigation in Honduras has not begun.

It is difficult to ever justify the denial of funding for the poor when we consider the faith-based moral mandate to do that as given to us by Our Lord. Representatives of MHI and the US Franciscans have declined to comment on why they oppose funding to aid the poor children of Honduras and the Dominican Republic.

Because the investigations can require lengthy periods, the lack of fundraising efforts in the United States has already resulted in hundreds and could result in thousands of children in the poorest countries in the world being deprived of food, shelter and education. Even the best of well intended procedures can have devastating effects in some circumstances.

In early January, 2010, the USCCB was asked to review this case. In their response the Office of the Secretariat of Child and Youth Protection noted, "The mandate of the USCCB's Secretariat of Child and Youth Protection is to address the issue of clergy sexual abuse within the U.S. Catholic Church, and this issue falls outside that purview". In addition to the dubious restriction on funding, this response raises the issue as to the degree, if any, religious orders domiciled in the United States should be involved when sexual abuses occur in foreign countries, which are operated by secular foreign-based missionary organizations even though they may be funded wholly or partially by US charitable organizations.

It was my belief that, initially, all parties were trying to do what they believed to be morally correct. Those involved in the Church, who cut off funding, were trying to comply with the rules made by human beings. The problem was that in applying such rules they violated the teaching of our Lord.

If love and kindness had prevailed the pursuit of both goals could have taken place—a safer environment for the children—while also maintaining the funding to permit the feeding and education of the children.

It has been a faith-based moral injustice to have the poor children deprived of a better life. It has also been disappointing, that those who were informed of the violation of our Lord's teaching by cutting off the funding, have for the past several years refused to change their position. These include members of the Church hierarchy, who undoubtedly understand the teachings of our Lord, but for reasons that are unknown to me refuse to revoke or amend the endorsement against the funding needed to help the poor children in Honduras.

It is impossible for me to reconcile their approval or abetment to obstruct funding for the poor children with our Lord's admonishment to the Pharisees that their rules and procedures needed to be applied in a loving, kind, merciful, and compassionate manner. It is difficult to understand the faith-based morality of their decisions to place their rules and procedures above the gospels and the unmistakable teachings of our Lord regarding the poor.

At a time when the Church in the United States is very properly concerned about the government forcing Church organizations to comply with immoral mandates in regards to providing contraceptive medications or devices to women, they have chosen a poor time to be guilty of taking morally questionable action against the poor children of Honduras. Our Lord often reminded the Pharisees against hypocrisy. It is wrong for the government to mandate Church organizations to violate their beliefs, and it is also wrong for those in position of authority within the

Church to violate the teaching of our Lord as regards the poor.

However, someone within the hierarchy of the Church in Honduras has taken a different view than those within the US Church hierarchy. Oscar Andres Cardinal Rodriguez Maradiaga, whose love and care of the poor is well known on a worldwide basis, in a letter to this writer promised that he would do whatever he could to come to the aid of the children who are being denied the opportunity for a better life.

Cardinal Rodriguez is the current President of Caritas International and with his distinguished reputation for helping the poor, there is reason to believe that he will do what is within his power to mitigate the damage done through the discouragement of funding imposed in his country. But he also wrote this writer that his promise to help as much as he can will not be easy. As he indicated, the position taken by the Conventual Franciscans and the circulation of the non-endorsement of funding circulated on behalf of the Franciscans by the United States Conference of Catholic Bishops will make his job difficult.

Central American countries are provided some financial assistance from this nation and from US Catholic organizations. The USCCB is a powerful group and can influence contributions made to foreign countries. One can understand that Cardinal Rodriquez' concerns must go beyond the single issue of the poor children being aided by APUFRAM.

It is my belief that our Lord permits injustices to occur so a greater good will result. It is not apparent as yet what that greater good will entail but we can be confident that our Lord's love for the poor children of Honduras will prevail. Sometimes that love must come after our life on earth is over.

Before the Cardinal's involvement, there were other faithful people who would not permit the abandonment of the poor children of Honduras. The one who sacrificed and suffered most for his beloved children was undoubtedly Father Emil.

Father Emil Cook would be dismissed from his Order, but he continued to do everything he possibly could to raise funds for his beloved poor children. Largely due to his efforts, there are hundreds of children that can be fed and educated annually. Unfortunately the funding has been inadequate to care for additional hundreds of children because some facilities have been shuttered.

Father Emil now continues his priestly work under the guidance of Cardinal Rodriguez. He made the difficult choice that it was more important for him to continue helping the poor children of Honduras than to remain a Conventual Franciscan. He is not the first laborer in the Lord's vineyard who needed to make a difficult choice. Saints John of the Cross, Theodore Guerin, Faustina Kowalska, Mary MacKillop and many others have also been misunderstood by members of the hierarchy within our beloved Church. They also had to endure great sacrifices in their pursuit of God's work on earth. But their love of our Lord's teachings enabled them to continue his work, despite the sacrifices demanded of them. The work done by Father Emil Cook also required great love of our Lord and great sacrifice. He has done much for the people of Honduras, especially the poor children of that country.

APUFRAM, the Honduran organization founded by Father Emil continues to operate and care for the aforementioned hundreds of children each year. They have done what they can do with the funds available to care for and love the poor. They have also instituted more rigorous child protection standards than were in place when the incident in Liberia occurred. Some members of their organization were alleged to have participated in sexual misconduct but none of those charges have ever been proven or even been pursued. Even if one or several individuals within the organization did not live up to the trust placed in them, their transgressions should not have deprived hundreds of children each year from receiving food and an education.

With recent developments in this case it now appears unlikely that such charges will ever be pursued and the restriction on funding will likely remain as a sad legacy to the injustice of this case and of the lack of love, mercy and compassion desired by the teaching of our Lord. If today, such charges are not worthy of investigation, it is difficult to understand why they were made.

A new organization in the United States, APUFRAM International, was created to help provide financial support for APUFRAM. Their efforts and those of Father Emil are hampered by the non-funding endorsement of the hierarchy of the Church in the United States. This organization and some supporters, who are dedicated to helping the poor, continue to solicit funds from a base of donors, despite the funding obstacles endorsed by hierarchical members within the Church.

There is no doubt that this case has caused sacrifice and suffering to Father Emil and the good members of APUFRAM. It will probably never be known if any of the accusations made against some of their members were justified. But their good work for poor children speaks volumes of their faith in our Lord, as does the efforts of the people who operate and donate to APUFRAM International.

None of the people I have come to know in those organizations are haphazard in their support of a safe environment for the children, but they also understand that faith in our Lord extends to loving those poor children of Honduras who have been abandoned by others.

It is difficult to understand why anyone would endorse a position that is harmful to poor children, but in this case they probably believed it would somehow aid in bringing a safer environment to the children of Honduras. This case demonstrates the spiritual warfare that was noted at the beginning of this chapter.

The process that resulted in the non-endorsement of funding was the result of following certain procedures of the religious Order and standards of the United States Conference of Catholic Bishops. Those procedures and standards relate to sexual abuse by priests in this country and did not apply to this case. They were applied in a manner that has deprived and will continue to deprive a large number of the poorest of the poor children in Honduras the opportunity for a better life. Sadly, it is not only governments that harm the poor.

If the admonitions of our Lord to the Pharisees to be a loving, kind, merciful and compassionate people when administering their rules had been followed in this case, the non-endorsement of funding would not have taken place. The example and words of our Lord should not be subordinated to words that are contained in constitutions, standards, rules and procedures that have been written by humans. If a conflict occurs the words of our Lord should dictate the action our faith in Him commands.

The lesson of this case should be that which our Lord was trying to convey to the woman who wished to bless His mother. More blessed are those who hear his words and observe them. The observation of his words lead us to a life of greater faith and thereby a greater observance of living in accord with faith-based morality. That type of morality stretches beyond things of this earth. It stretches to eternity. Many in this case have sacrificed and suffered in order to extend their love to those who are also greatly loved by our Lord.

Our Lord's admonitions to the Pharisees are admonitions that are intended for all of us. When conflicts occur, which can be resolved by following the words taught us by our Lord, the path we should take is clear. He taught us that such conflicts can be eliminated by mercy, love, compassion and kindness. We are all human beings made in the image and likeness of our Creator. Our Lord loves all of us and most assuredly the poor children in the poor country of Honduras. Much spiritual warfare can be resolved when we truly hear and observe his words.

CHAPTER 11

THE PAIN AND LOVE OF MOTHERS

The women of the world have a wonderful role model in the Blessed Virgin Mary. Her whole life was a lesson in the dedication of love to our Lord. With the words, "Behold the handmaid of the Lord, be it done unto me according to thy words", she committed her entire life to that love of God. She would endure pregnancy and the pain of giving birth in a stable to become the Mother of God.

She would endure much suffering for the love of her Son. After giving birth in the stable, she with her devoted husband, Joseph, would flee to Egypt to escape the death of her Son by Herod. She would see Him carry his Cross to Calvary and there be crucified for the sins of others. Her love was great and so would be her rewards as she became the Queen of Heaven and Earth.

As the mother of God she shared a special bond with her divine Son. Her words at the wedding feast in Cana were the last words ascribed to her in Holy Scripture, "Do what He tells you". They were not only words to the winemakers, but are words for all of us on earth to heed. She was devoted to Him in his divinity.

But she also shared a special bond with her human Son. She gave birth as other women give birth on earth. She understood the concerns of other women for their children when she and Joseph searched for Him at the age of twelve as He was speaking to the elders in the Temple. She grieved for Him as He carried the Cross to Calvary. She stood at the foot of the Cross as He died for others. She helped lay Him in the tomb. She endured more than only the human pains of motherhood.

It is impossible for me to understand fully the bond that exists between a mother and her child. I am a man and did not have to undergo the pains of childbirth. It has been said frequently that there is no greater pain on earth than that experienced by a mother giving birth. But as soon as that birth is consummated, a special bond takes place between mother and child. In many ways that bond starts at conception.

It is not only a bond that is established but also a very special love that takes place. Can we say it is the love created from the pain of giving birth? Maybe we don't fully understand the special love that takes place between mother and child but we know it exists.

It is unfortunate that in our nation as well as other nations, the elevation of rights for women was accompanied to some degree by the diminishment of the very important role of motherhood. The role of the mother is one of the most important roles human beings can play while on earth. It is through the nurturing care of a mother that future good citizens evolve.

But, of even more importance than the role mothers play to see that their children become good citizens, is the role they along with fathers play, in preparing children for their place in the Kingdom God has prepared for us. The mercy and compassion of a mother and the justice taught by a father are tremendously important in preparing children for their eternal reward in Heaven. Parents have no greater role than to instill a love of God in their children. That role requires patience and love along with great sacrifice.

In the January, 2013 issue of "Living with Christ" the following was stated: *The Dalai Lama once remarked that we receive our first lessons in peaceful living from our mothers, who reveal for us what love is and does. Their loving care for us in our helplessness establishes the foundation for creating right relationships in the family, in society and among nations.* Such love comes with the many sacrifices and sufferings a mother makes for her children.

The sacrifice of a good mother means subordinating much of her own time and her own activities to that of her children. Loving our neighbor as our self begins at home. She is psychologist, nurse, activities director, moral instructor and many other functions to her children.

In the world we live in today the special bond that will exist between mother and child, is too frequently not permitted to exist because the child is aborted. That woman is forever deprived of that special love. But the soul of that aborted child will not be forsaken by our Lord as was noted in Chapter 8.

It is difficult for us on earth to comprehend the meeting of the soul of the aborted child. with the soul of its mother in life hereafter. Maybe that meeting will not be permitted by our Lord to ever take place. We do not know. The mere thought of that is an indication of an even greater pain the mother who succumbs to an abortion may experience in life after death. But that decision will be made by our Lord and he is a forgiving and loving God and with Him that reconciliation too is possible.

An expectant mother on earth can take great comfort from the wonderful blessing that she is permitted to experience the birth of a child as was experienced by the Blessed Mother of Jesus.

Much about the duration of a pregnancy involves pain. Mothers go through "morning sickness" and then experience considerable discomfort through the course of pregnancy. And finally there is the pain of childbirth. But almost all mothers immediately after childbirth feel and understand the love for their child and that they have had the privilege of being a part of God's plan for humans. Life begins with pain for the mother and life often ends with pain.

Mothers who experience great pain in childbirth can take much comfort in knowing that giving life to a new human being can be unifying with the pain our Lord suffered on the Cross when He gave all humans the potential life of eternal happiness.

Motherhood is a special privilege. It produces a special love. It requires pain and sacrifice. But the result is great love.

CHAPTER 12

SPIRITUAL LOVE

Love is a word that gets much use. But too frequently it becomes a word that is used without sincerity. Sincere, heartfelt, spiritual love truly is the greatest of all virtues that we humans possess.

St. John the Evangelist and St. Paul frequently spoke of love. St. Paul in his first letter to the Corinthians gave us both the importance of love and a great definition of spiritual love.

If I speak in human and angelic tongues but do not have love, I am a resounding gong or a clashing cymbal. And if I have the gift of prophecy and comprehend all mysteries and all knowledge; if I have all faith so as to move mountains but do not have love I am nothing. If I give away everything I own, and if I hand my body over so that I may boast but do not have love, I gain nothing.

Love is patient, love is kind. It is not jealous, (love) is not pompous, it is not inflated, it is not rude, it does not seek its own interests, it is not quick-tempered, it does not brood over injury. it does not rejoice over wrongdoing but rejoices with the truth. It bears all things, believes all things, hopes all things, endures all things.

Love never fails . . . So faith, hope, love remain, these three; but the greatest of these is love.

To love in the manner St. Paul describes is not easy. During his time on earth our Lord demonstrated the optimal love that can be achieved. His passion and crucifixion on behalf of sinners is almost beyond comprehension. He died not just for those who would love him but also for those who, do not know Him, despise Him, and reject his teachings. It is a spiritual love that cannot be replicated by flawed humans during their time on earth.

It seems paradoxical that we are asked by our Lord to love one another as He loves us while knowing that it is not possible to do that while we are on earth. But we can be consoled by the words our Lord spoke of St. John the Baptist that were also noted in Chapter 3. *No one born of woman is greater than John, but as great as he was, he was not as great as the least of those in the Kingdom of God.*

In Chapter 3, we attempted to explain why Jesus spoke those words of John. While he was on earth John was still subjected to sin. Sin is a repudiation of God's love. Since John was still capable of sin while on earth he was incapable of loving God as God loved him. But if in this life we do our best to love Him, we will be preparing ourselves for the greater experience of loving Him even more when we reach our Heavenly home.

Our Lord, in his perfection, understood that the commands he gave us were indeed somewhat paradoxical. Nevertheless he gave us the teachings and commandments that were necessary for us on earth to attempt to achieve that perfect spiritual love even though we cannot achieve it. Our purpose on earth is to continue to attempt to achieve that great spiritual love, we cannot fully achieve.

He gave us the two greatest commandments of how we are to live our lives on earth. *You shall love the Lord, your God, with all your heart, with all your soul, and with all your mind. This is the first commandment. The second is like it: You shall love your neighbor as yourself. The whole law and the prophets depend on these two commandments.*

Our never-ending purpose is to attempt to comply with these two commands, even though they are commands that also are not fully achievable by those of us on earth. If they were achievable on earth the prayer he taught us "Your will be done on earth as it is in Heaven" would be accomplished. Thus the closer we on earth come to complying with his commands the closer we will be to having Heaven on earth.

We need to remember the words of St. Paul—that of faith, hope and love the greatest is love.

When each of us are prepared to suffer and die as He did for each of us, it will be the time we come closest to emulating the great spiritual love He has for us.

In his encyclical on Love of God, Pope Benedict XVI spoke beautifully of how we must work to achieve a greater love and of its importance:

The love-story between God and man consists in the very fact that this communion of will increases in a communion of thought and sentiment, and thus our will and God's will increasingly coincide . . .

Love is difficult. It goes against the egotistical nature of our human mind. Our flawed nature makes it impossible to some degree. But it is not impossible to keep trying. In the Prologue of the Roman Catholic Church Catechism we are told:

The whole concern of doctrine and its teaching must be directed to the love that never ends. Whether something is proposed for belief, for hope or for action, the love of our Lord must always be made accessible, so that everyone can see that all the works of perfect Christian virtue spring from love and have no other objective than to arrive at love.

Those words fortify what St. Paul also told us. Our life on earth must be a constant effort to have no greater objective than to arrive at that perfect spiritual love albeit not achievable during our time on earth. But the best effort to achieve it will be the best road we can follow to join Him in his Kingdom.

Let us now turn to the messages Scripture has provided for us in order to help us attempt to achieve that great love of which St. Paul spoke.

In Chapter 5 of Matthew, verses 43 to 48 Jesus told us; *You have heard that it was said, 'You shall love your neighbor and hate your enemy.' But I say to you, love your enemies, and pray for those who persecute you, that you may be children of your heavenly Father, for he makes his sun rise on the bad and the good, and causes rain to fall on the just and the unjust. For if you love those who love you, what recompense will you have? Do not the tax collectors do the same? And if you greet your brothers only, what is unusual about that? Do not the pagans do the same? So be perfect, just as your Heavenly Father is perfect.*

As noted earlier, love is not easy and great spiritual love is extremely difficult but that is what Jesus is asking of us. Love the serial killer, love the child abuser, love the ruthless dictator and love all who seem to reject the word of God. We do not know the minds and hearts of others so we must let God make the judgment of justice. Only He knows the innermost thoughts of our "enemies".

In John 13, verses 34-35, Jesus gave his disciples and us a new commandment regarding love:

I give you a new commandment: love one another. As I have loved you, so you also should love one another. This is how all will know that you are my disciples, if you have love for one another.

As good Christians we pray for greater faith, hope and love. These are great virtues and important for all of us to obtain the eternal salvation earned for us by the passion and death of our Lord. As St. Paul told us the greatest of these is love.

Let us then examine why spiritual love is the greatest of all virtues. Faith and hope are of tremendous importance for us as we go through the spiritual battle during our life on earth. It is a spiritual battle, because the sins of the body pull us all too frequently in the wrong direction whereas the Spirit (soul) pulls us toward the spiritual love our Lord asked of us.

But at the end of life on earth the body returns to dust and the soul continues throughout eternity. After we pass from this earth faith and hope are no longer a necessity. They were the virtues whereby the human mind was led to a life that will gain us salvation.

But love remains. It is THE virtue that will remain with us through eternity. It is the virtue that we must work to perfect in this life.

We do not know what God has ready for those who love Him, but we do know that love will remain

CHAPTER 13

THE EXPECTATIONS OF OUR LORD

An often repeated warning our Lord made to the Pharisees was the need to administer laws in a loving, kind, merciful and compassionate manner. That admonishment was not only intended for the Pharisees of that time. To the degree that we are all sinners we need to take his warning personally. All of us at some time or another are guilty of acting in a manner that is not loving, kind, merciful or compassionate. We are human beings who are flawed. We are humble beings that find it difficult to love our neighbor as our self. We are humans beings who too often believe our way is the right and sometimes only way.

Yes, our Lord's warnings to the Pharisees were not just for the Pharisees but for all of us. In Chapter 10, a sad story is noted of what unnecessarily happened to thousands of poor children in Honduras. One of the unfortunate and sad parts of that story is the failure of those within the Church to undo the damage done to the children they assisted in harming. All of us are guilty at times of saying: "It is not my problem"—"We must abide by our policies"—"I am too busy with other problems"— "I would like to help but I don't have the time". In the process we subordinate the wishes and commands of our Lord. What was done to the least of those children was done to Him.

Our Lord expects us to be full-time Christians and not just when it is convenient for us. Because of our sinful and egotistical nature, it is not easy to be at all times a loving, kind, merciful and compassionate person, but that is what our Lord expects of us.

He who suffered and died so we might have eternal happiness has every right to expect that and more of us. He did not say that it was too humbling for Him to come to earth to live among us, but he could have. He did not tell his Father that suffering and dying for an ungrateful people was unnecessary but He could have. He could have done all those things and more but He did not. Why? He loved us more than we will ever be able to love Him during our time on earth, but he expects us to make that effort.

How can we improve our efforts to increase our love for the Lord? It must be our highest priority in life. It must be an understanding that the distractions of life on earth must be minimized so our love of Him can be maximized through the realization that our love of Him will be the only thing that matters once we complete our time on earth.

Love of God is not always easy for us to explain or to understand. It is our never-ending goal on earth to live so we may increase that love. To perfect that love demands the winning of a spiritual warfare within us whereby we must constantly overcome the temptations of the world and of our own flesh.

We can do no better describing "love" than to repeat the words in Chapter 4 verses 7-21 of the First Letter of John: *Beloved, let us love one another, because love is of God; everyone who loves is begotten by God and knows God. Whoever is without love does not know God, for God is love. In this way the love of God was revealed to us: GOD SENT HIS ONLY SON INTO THE WORLD SO THAT WE MIGHT HAVE LIFE THROUGH HIM. IN THIS IS LOVE; NOT THAT WE HAVE LOVED GOD, BUT THAT HE LOVED US AND SENT HIS SON AS EXPIATION FOR OUR SINS. Beloved, if God so loved us, we must also love one another. No one has ever seen God. Yet, if we love one another, God remains in us, and his love is brought to perfection in us.*

This is how we know that we remain in him and he in us, that he had given us of his Spirit. Moreover, we have seen and testify that the Father sent his Son as savior of the world. Whoever acknowledges that Jesus is the Son of God, God remains in him and he in God. We have come to know and to believe in the love God has for us.

God is love, and whoever remains in love remains in God and God in him. In this is love brought to perfection among us, that we have confidence on the day of judgment because as he is, so are we in this world.

There is no fear in love, but perfect love drives out fear because fear has to do with punishment, and so one who fears is not yet perfect in love. We love because he first loved us. If anyone says, "I love God," but hates his brother, he is a liar: for whoever does not love a brother whom he has seen cannot love God whom he has not seen. This is the commandment we have from him: whoever loves God must also love his brother.

The above words are easy to read but are not so easy to live. As noted earlier the temptations of this world and the temptations of our human body cause a conflict with that perfect love John describes. In order to work toward that perfect love we must also work toward a more perfect humility, because we cannot love our God and brother if we love our self more.

We must start each day with the dedication that the day will be one of offering all our prayers, works, sufferings, offerings and joys of the day to Him who suffered and died for us. His example of love and sacrifice must be the example we follow and live. It is not easy to love our enemies but that is what God commanded us to do.

We must learn to love the terrorist, the child molester, the murderer, and all sinners on earth as God loved them. It is not our job on earth to judge but rather to love. In so doing, we must block out the prejudices created in our own sinful mind and try harder to adopt the love of which John spoke. Our Lord gave his life for all of us, even those who did, do, and will despise

Him and his teachings. To love our brother as He loved us means we must be prepared to do the same.

The perfection of love is a never ending process. Because we are sinners, we will fail from time to time. That does not mean we should give up. It means we should repent and resolve to do better in the future. We live in a sinful world and we live in a body stained by original sin. That for which we strive will not be achieved on this earth, but we must not be deterred from our efforts to achieve that perfect love.

He also gave us a method whereby we can help ourselves toward that more perfect love. He taught us how to pray. It is through prayer that we can help ourselves. As we learn to better praise and glorify Him through prayer we will also learn more of His great love for us. As we learn the great love He had for us, we will be better able to love as He expected us to love.

His command to each of us and his expectation was simply stated: "Love one another as I have loved you". When we can see and love Jesus in everyone on this earth and leave all judgments of everyone on earth to Him who will also judge us, then we will be closer to his other simple statement; "Be Holy for I am Holy".

But to be Holy as He is Holy, requires a great sacrifice. We must think no more of ourselves than we think of others and we must think even more of Him. In order to increase love for our Lord and love of our neighbor the sacrifice of humility must be a daily and constant struggle

CHAPTER 14

THE NEED FOR HUMILITY

"It was pride that made angels into devils: it is humility that makes men as angels". That value of humility was expressed by St. Augustine. Our Lord made the value of humility even more clear in the Beatitudes; "Blessed are the meek, for they will inherit the earth".

If we wish to increase our faith in God and our love of God, we must also increase our humility. Therein, is the great spiritual sacrifice and struggle faced by all humans on earth. The spiritual struggle comes from the conflict between our body and soul.

Faith is a special gift from God. It is the understanding and acceptance of our Lord and his teachings and that He alone is responsible for our salvation. But the earthly pride of our human mind pulls us in the opposite direction.

The gift of faith is offered by God to all humans. It is up to the free will God has granted to humans as to whether or not they wish to accept that gift. If accepted, it is also up to each human being to decide how much they wish to grow that faith. The growth of that faith is dependent on an individual's willingness to sacrifice their own egos (false pride). That willingness comes from the soul within us and the acceptance of grace. Our Lord told us that "it is the spirit that gives life (faith and eternal salvation), while the flesh is of no avail".

Our Lord also gave us the two greatest commandments—one was to love Him above all else and two was to love our neighbor as our self. When we as humans are able to comply with those two commandments we also demonstrate great faith. But how many of us day in and day out comply perfectly with those commandments? The answer is that we don't. Our Lord understood perfectly well that we are sinners but He wanted us to do our very best to observe his commands and thereby grow our faith. In order to do that, we must have a great love of humility.

Humility requires sacrificing the desires of the human mind and flesh. Humility requires the rejection of the temptations of this earthly life. As we struggle to increase our humility, the more we will increase our spiritual wisdom and our love of God.

If we wish to emulate an example of great humility, we can find that example in our Lord and Savior. Our Lord came to earth as one of us. This was our God. This was the 2nd Person of the Blessed Trinity. And yet this was He who came to us as one of us—born in a manger and lived the life of a carpenter. As an infant He would live the life of a refugee in Egypt to escape Herod. He would not acquire the material possessions that other humans strive to possess. He was indeed meek and humble of heart.

He would humble Himself even more through his passion and death. He endured the sentence of death despite committing no crime. He was scourged at the pillar and beaten. He permitted humans to place a crown of thorns on Him. He carried a Cross for people who sinned against Him. He walked with the Cross to the place of his crucifixion without complaining. He was stripped of his garments—the last of his earthly possessions. He permitted Himself to be nailed to a cross and crucified. He permitted these things even though He was our God. As God, He did not need to suffer the greatest of all humiliations—passion and death. But He did it for love of us.

Yes, if we want an example of humility, our Lord demonstrated it from the day of his birth to his death on the Cross. He gave us that example by showing how the love of others could and should be the objective of one's life. And therein is humility. When we can subordinate thoughts of our self and elevate our life and love for others, as He did for us, then we experience the humility that also makes it possible to increase the love of our Lord.

That type of humility for humans demands a sacrifice that is simply impossible for sinners to maintain at all times. Even the best of humans failed. The cock crowed three times for St. Peter. St. Paul persecuted those who loved our Lord. Jesus noted that as great as John the Baptist was, he was not as great as the least of those in Heaven. Yes, we will fail at times. Our Lord understands that, but he wants us to try. "Be perfect as the Heavenly Father is perfect".

While we are on earth, we cannot be as perfect as our Heavenly Father, but we can strive each day to be more perfect and more humble. We can awaken each day and resolve to spend that day loving God more and our neighbor as our self. We can do our best during the course of the day to be meek and to think in accordance with the words of the song "a little more of my neighbor and a little less of me". When we achieve these things we make the world a better place and making the world a better place begins with us. We also begin preparing our soul a little better for its ultimate goal—Heaven.

Humility does not demand that we refuse to use the talents we receive from God. St. Paul indicated that in his letter to the Romans. *For by the grace given to me I tell everyone among you not to think of himself more highly than one ought to think, but to think soberly, each according to the measure of faith that God has apportioned. For as in one body we have many parts, and all the parts do not have the same function, so we, though many, are one body in Christ and individually parts of one another. Since we have gifts that differ according to the grace given to us, let us exercise them: if prophecy, in proportion to the faith: if ministry, in ministering; if one is a teacher, in teaching: if one exhorts, in exhortation; if one contributes, in generosity: if one is over others, with diligence; if one does acts of mercy, with cheerfulness.*

Humility does not require that we withdraw from the world. Humility is eliminating the false pride which causes us to think more of our self than we think of God or neighbor.

It is through greater humility that we are able to have greater faith and through greater faith we increase our love of God and neighbor. Humility does require sacrifice and through humility we are better able to accept suffering. As noted in this book, many who loved God greatly were also subjected to great pain and even death. Our martyrs and saints who suffered greatly during their time on earth can be our role models in how to increase our humility, our faith and our love. If we can increase our humility, we can better accept the suffering we may have to endure on earth.

The greatest role model of all is our Savior. He accepted humanity, passion and suffering for the greatest love ever demonstrated on earth. In so doing he humbled himself greatly. His example on earth of great humility through sacrifice and suffering can be a constant reminder that our greater love can be achieved through greater sacrifice and suffering.

Pain and sacrifice present a dichotomy for humans. On the one hand we pray for those who are suffering that they be relieved of their pain. On the other hand we acknowledge that it was through our Lord's suffering and death that he demonstrated his ultimate love for us. We can become more united with our Redeemer's great love for us, when through our own suffering and sacrifice, we endure it for Him who accepted it for us so we might enjoy eternity with Him.

ABOUT THE AUTHOR

George E Pfautsch spent most of his working life as a financial executive for a major forest products and paper company. His final years at Potlatch Corporation were spent as the Senior Vice-President of Finance and Chief Financial Officer. Following his retirement, he began writing and speaking about the national morality he believes was intended for this nation by the founding fathers of the country. He is the author of seven previous books on the subjects of morality, justice and faith. He is the co-author of a book written by Melitta Strandberg, which is the story of her family's quest for freedom, before, during and after World War II. He is also the co-author of a book written by Leroy New, the "Guitar Wizard" of Branson, Missouri. He is married to Dodi, his wife of 51 years. He has two children and four grandchildren.